Contents

An inexpert Guide to Allotment Gardening	3
Copyright Page:	4
Author Bio	5
Introduction:	6
A is for Arrival	9
B is for Brassicas	12
C is for Community	15
D is for Disease and Pests	18
E is for Experiments	22
F is for Fertilisers	27
G is for Greenhouse	31
H is for Harvest Time	34
I is for Improvement	38
J is for Journal	40
K is for Kitchen Gardening	42
L is for Low Maintenance	46
M is for Mental Health	49
N is for Nature	52
O is for Organic	55
P is for Pollinators	58

Q is for Quarantine	62
R is for Roots	65
S is for Soil	68
T is for tools	71
U is for Unusual	74
V is for Variety	78
W is for Weather	81
X is for Xeriscaping and Irrigation	83
Y is for Youths	86
Z is for Zones	90
GLOSSARY	92
Acknowledgments	94

A-Z
of
Allotment Gardening

Our 1st Year : The Lockdown Edition

An inexpert Guide to Allotment Gardening

Written by S K Garrod

Photos by S K Garrod

A – Z of Allotment Gardening © Copyright <<2020>> Sophie Garrod

All rights reserved. No part of this publication may be reproduced, distributed or transmitted in any form or by any means, including photocopying, recording, or other electronic or mechanical methods, without the prior written permission of the publisher, except in the case of brief quotations embodied in critical reviews and certain other non-commercial uses permitted by copyright law.

Although the author and publisher have made every effort to ensure that the information in this book was correct at press time, the author and publisher do not assume and hereby disclaim any liability to any party for any loss, damage, or disruption caused by errors or omissions, whether such errors or omissions result from negligence, accident, or any other cause.

Adherence to all applicable laws and regulations, including international, federal, state and local governing professional licensing, business practices, advertising, and all other aspects of doing business in the US, Canada or any other jurisdiction is the sole responsibility of the reader and consumer.

Neither the author nor the publisher assumes any responsibility or liability whatsoever on behalf of the consumer or reader of this material. Any perceived slight of any individual or organization is purely unintentional.

The resources in this book are provided for informational purposes only and should not be used to replace the specialized training and professional judgment of a health care or mental health care professional.

Neither the author nor the publisher can be held responsible for the use of the information provided within this book. Please always consult a trained professional before making any decision regarding treatment of yourself or others.

For more information, email sophie.elvin@yahoo.co.uk

Author Bio

At age 32, a jerk reaction decision to become an Allotment owner had more life changing effects than Sophie could have hoped for. In all her history she had never shown any interest in gardening, but within a few months she had managed to turn a plot of grass into a fully functioning allotment. Providing the family with an abundance of food within a matter of weeks, as well as teaching the children valuable life skills and making some amazing memories.

The inspirational journey from nimble fingered to green fingered has been captured in her A-Z of Allotment Gardening. This book demonstrates how Sophie, her husband and her three little boys have explored gardening during the Coronavirus Pandemic in the UK. When the world was full of doom and gloom, they found a way to have fun whilst learning, becoming self-sufficient and helping the planet in their own little ways.

Introduction:

Finally, I get to sit down, take 5 minutes, and do the only thing that is known to modern man, scroll through Social Media. After almost 9 weeks of being in Lockdown, I have completely run out of the initial enthusiasm I began with. I'm not entirely sure where it all went, but perhaps the daily battle with 3 kids to get some Home Schooling done, then the unvarying woodland walk with the dog (it began by taking some 'Fun' worksheets to do whilst there, but now it's more of a chore. Plus, the whole village has found the woods now and it isn't a quiet place anymore) and then the after-lunch slog of "What can we do now?". Mostly, the answer to that is "Nothing kids, we are locked down and everywhere is closed".

Going back to putting my feet up, the most exciting part of my day at present, I am scrolling through the social media newsfeed, and up pops a new status from my friend. They have just acquired an allotment, in a village not so far away. Cue the brainwave, an allotment, the cure to all lockdown evil!

I may have mentioned already that I have 3 delightful little boys, George, Harry, and Alfie. The eldest of the rabble is George, having just started High School. With the abundance of attitude and hormones bubbling away, he would happily sit on social media all day long. My efforts to entertain George have failed miserably; he no longer enjoys crafts or toys, but prefers computer games and football. There is no need for social interaction with Mum or his brothers

The middle cherub is Harry, just 20 months younger than George; he has not become a stereotypical teenager just yet. Harry enjoys the outdoors (when I can get him motivated), but he also prefers football and computer games. Happy to interact with his little brother still and seems to enjoy most things once motivated.

The final Musketeer is little Alfie, the baby in the family having just started his second year at School. Alfie is solely built for the great outdoors, he has been labelled with ADHD and Autism, but it does not hold this dude back! If you can find a pile of muck or a bucket of worms, Alfie is right there beside it.

Now you know the ins and outs of my daily life at the present time, you may understand why an Allotment would be the greatest gift on earth at this moment. In case you do not understand why, I will happily let you in on the secret. These boys do not enjoy this home schooling malarky that has been thrust upon us all. Although I am intelligent, I was never destined to be a teacher. My efforts to engage them and make education fun, has fallen on deaf ears. An allotment would be the answer, learning whilst having genuine fun; they may not even notice they are learning due to having so much fun?! The motivational boost of getting to go outside and explore, digging, getting grubby and we could even bring the dog and save the woods from our multitude of charming walks! We would be in our own little Covid secure bubble of muck.

The idea has been sold, no need to discuss or share with anyone just yet, because I need to act fast. Let the emails and phone calls commence, so exciting, I am sure we will have our own little patch of ground in no time. But little did I know, I am slow to the Allotment idea and most sites now have an exceptionally long waiting list. Never one to give up though, I keep on trying, calling every council within a 10-mile radius. It is amazing how many allotment sites are around us, that I have never acknowledged before.

Just as I am about to give up and resign myself to the fact we will not have our dream patch of muck for the Summer, I get a return call from the site that my friend has just been accepted on. They have a quarter sized plot available and we can begin ownership within the week! Now to break the news of the century to my husband and the trio of trouble.

So, there it is, our brief and extremely motivating journey into why and how we came to be the lovely owners of an Allotment.

A is for Arrival

Within a few hours of receiving the phone call to confirm our allotment, we were standing in the middle of our very own patch of grass in the middle of a windy field. The reality began to sink in, but the excitement levels were rising.

For a minimal cost per year, we could make this happen. I had no idea where to start and certainly no previous gardening experience to go by. It was time to seek advice from all those around me with the knowledge to help us start our gardening journey. My Mum, Dad, Nanny, In-laws, and local community were all on hand to help and soon the dreams would become reality.

It was quickly apparent that the Allotment site was going through a period of change and we were not the only newbies to the block. Along with my friend across the track, there were a few other new families and couples who had recently joined and were beginning their journeys also. It was reassuring to know that all the eyes were not just on us. The corner plot was called 'The Furlough', which I found very appropriate and amusing.

To begin with, our plot was a long, narrow patch of couch grass with a few sporadic strawberry's plants and a tangle of Raspberry canes in one corner. There was a path laid in bark chippings down one side and across the back, and an area in the corner with the odd paving stone laid. The initial layout was set, a shed would go nicely on the paving stones and a nice seating area across the back. We decided we would like to keep the Raspberries and condense the Strawberries in to one area.

It did not take long before we felt more confident about making the plot work. Many of the plot holders around ours gave us their spare seedlings, we picked up all the free pallets and such like that we saw advertised and we were grateful to be given lots of cuttings of flowers from my mum and neighbours.

The site is only a small one, comprising of just 28 plots. They run either side of a track, with a communal orchard in the middle. Everyone seemed very friendly and we soon became regulars, chatting with them all from a Covid safe distance and making friends. The children were keen to visit the allotment a few times a week and had plenty of ideas between them. It soon started to look more cultivated and the children were learning daily.

It was lovely to walk into an established site and see so many ideas for inspiration. Every plot full to the brim in peak growing season. The plots with flowers and scarecrows grabbed our attention, and we loved the beautiful peas and beans, that rose into the air like wigwams. It was right from the beginning that I decided we would have a plot to remember, one that people would like to stop and enjoy as they wandered past. The plots laid out in the manner of row upon row of crop were somewhat unappealing to me, we would create something unique and outside the box.

On one of our first wanders around the site, we were happily showing my mum and discussing ideas when we stumbled across a poor little fledgling that had become entangle in some strawberry netting. Although he was positioned inside another person's plot, we ventured in regardless and were able to rescue the bird. Luckily for him, we had some nail scissors in our handbag and managed to cut him free, he had obviously crept under the net to feast on some strawberries before getting caught when trying to exit. Thankfully he flew away unharmed from my mums grasp and we popped a little message to the plot holder to let her know what had happened. This was probably one of the first lessons I learnt, to keep netting taught and reduce the possibility of animals getting tangled.

As soon as we had the phone call offering us the plot, I knew that we would need to invest in a shed to store all the tools and equipment that an allotment required to be maintained. There is such a huge variety of garden storage available, from plastic storage benches to extravagant garden outhouses. The rules for our site would allow a shed no larger than 6 x 4ft and it must be located at the rear of the plot, where luckily we already had some slabs laid for a base. I assumed the previous occupier had a shed placed there before. It just so happened that soon after we got the plot, a man in the next village was selling his shed for a very reasonable price and with my dads help, it was soon erected on our plot.

There was a bit of fiasco with the shed, as I rang my husband to arrange collection in his van. He was however adamant that it would not fit inside his van and he arranged with his boss to borrow the larger truck to transport the shed. It was not until after an hour or so of wondering why it would not fit in his van, I realised I had told my husband it was 6 x 4 metres instead of feet. Whoops! It was funny but I was not his favourite person for a while.

Now, the shed is our base when we arrive on site. It is home to a lovely cosy storage bench, which we have often sat on in the rain and enjoyed a picnic. I have added a couple of canvases with pretty landscapes, an essential clock for the days I need to combine gardening with school runs, a  shelving rack full of useful things like a staple gun and string and of course hooks along the walls for all the essential tools I have collected.

B is for Brassicas

These types of vegetables deserve their own chapter, because in my eyes, they are the nightmare vegetable to grow. However, they are worth the trouble as they are the powerhouse of the vegetable kingdom.

If you can get your Brassicas to grow and then to remain pest free, you are essentially able to eat the leaves, flowers, stems and roots; making them a super veg! But that is where the excitement ended for me. The first seedlings I was given were Purple Cauliflower, and they looked amazing. As a total novice to vegetable gardening, I did not realise the importance of researching how to in fact grow a plant before sowing it in the ground.

Hastily I tucked the Cauliflower seedlings into their cosy and warm soil bed, gave them some water and off home I went. Feeling so proud, it was heart wrenching when I returned to the plot the following day and saw a whole bed of stubbly green shoots. Obviously, the Pigeons enjoyed the sumptuous buffet I had laid out for them the day before! With this newfound information regarding plants and Pigeons, I thought I would be one step ahead and cover the Cauliflowers in a netting. Completely bird proof, and it worked!

After providing the Pigeons dinner, sadly 2 of the seedlings did not survive, but at least I had done my part for the local wildlife. Feeling smug, the remaining seedlings kept on growing and the children were fascinated when 2 of them developed stunning purple Cauliflower heads. I had never actually seen purple Cauliflowers, so was a bit hesitant when deciding whether to devour them for our tea or not.

The children were keen, and I am not one to back away from new experiences, so we pulled the only two fully grown Cauli-

flowers and bought them home. However, I soon realised what my next mistake had been. Little did I know, there are two types of nettings; one to prevent the birds and one to prevent the bugs. We pulled the munched leaves off and discovered a whole little world of Caterpillars and eggs hidden inside. Apparently, those pretty, white Butterflies are not so gardener friendly after all.

Without wanting to discourage the children's willingness to eat their produce, I bravely rinsed the Cauliflowers repeatedly. These caterpillars were everywhere, so it came to the point where I pulled all the individual heads apart and handpicked each one. But it was worth it, they tasted amazing. The first Brassicas we had organically homegrown and we enjoyed eating them too.

Sadly, the Cauliflowers were not the only poor brassica experience we had, as I had also been given some brussel sprout seedlings. ~Even though we covered these appropriately, they never grew very much. After some googling and social media requests for help, it turns out that the seedlings should have been planted out straight away but because we had left them in the pot, they had merged into one bush like plant and didn't have the space to grow properly. Another lesson learnt!

The final Brassica we tried was Broccoli, but again, several attempts ended badly. The first seeds did not do anything, maybe the slugs got to them through the soil. The second batch grew rapidly one night and developed flowers, which I now know is called bolting. This happened because of the adverse weather conditions and fortunately was not our fault. The third attempts were growing nicely, and then overnight they got thousands of holes munched through them. As much as we tried, we could not find any evidence of Caterpillars or Slugs and were quite stumped.

Then someone mentioned Fleas to us! Who knew there were fleas that ate vegetables! So that was the end of our final Broccoli attempt.

The broccoli that bolted was not left for waste though. After closer inspection, whilst pulling it all up we discovered it was absolutely riddled with pretty caterpillars. There must have been easily over fifty on each plant. It would be a shame to just throw these all into the compost bin so instead, we took some of them home and hatched them into a butterfly kit we have stored away. It was amazing to watch them grow and form chrysalis. They turned out to be what we think were Box Hedge Moths.
As the release of the moths loomed, we read in a magazine about the Big Butterfly Count. It is a nation-wide count for 15 minutes, in a sunny patch of your garden or allotment. The children enjoyed taking part in this count and we were surprised at how many varieties of butterflies relied upon our allotment for food and shelter.

Now I hope I have not put you off, as we will certainly be attempting to grow Brassicas again. All these lessons learnt can be put forward to help us create the best possible crops next time. Now we know that planning and preparation is far more important to prevent things from going wrong, and researching each plant is an important process to achieve its full potential.

C is for Community

This chapter is a vital part of the Allotment story, because with the community, our journey would have been a lot more difficult.

From the first day, we were greeted in the car park by a fellow Allotmenteer, and it has happened almost every visit since. There is always someone about to give a wave and a smile, and often, a quick catch-up and a chat.

During the Summer months, when it was terribly hot and dry, it seemed the community was brought together in means of a queue for the water taps. Everyone wanted to connect their hose and give their plots a good soaking at the same time. Thank goodness a second tap has been installed ready for next Summer, as some days we spent over an hour waiting to use it. On some days though, my friend and I would take turns in watering each other's plots as well as our own, saving a trip out in the sweltering heat.

Out of the blue, we would often have little seedlings left on our plot for us and this really helped us get established. Having left it later in the season to begin growing our Veg, these kind offerings made the world of difference. At Times, we had no idea what they were, and it was a lovely surprise when they started growing into plants we could identify. We happened to plant some grass looking seedlings, which turned out to be Sweetcorn and we really enjoyed them. The only problem with not knowing what they are, is not knowing how to plant them. The Sweetcorn for example, should be planted into grids, so they can pollinate each other easily but we planted out 4 seedlings in a pretty row and subsequently, only the top 4 cobs were pollinated properly. We did not let the rest go to waste though, they were hung on the bird table and enjoyed by a very appreciative little Robin.

The children have made some friends on the site a few plots down from ours, and this is great because during Lockdown, there were not many opportunities for them to practice their social skills. It also gave me time to concentrate on the gardening whilst they were playing; socially distanced of course.

Our site has its own Facebook Group, so we can discuss and share things on there too. It has been nice seeing other people's ideas and being able to ask advice. Many times, I have used social media for advice, but often I receive information from people in completely different zones and the advice is not always beneficial for the UK. I also find that the other plot holders on our site understand our soil type, wind issues and such like, so they can give advice from their personal experiences.

However, it has not always been great to have a lot of other plot holders about. Like the time I did the classic mistake of standing on the end of the rake, for it to ping up and knock me square in the nose! This was bad enough, but then I heard a bunch of giggling from all the witnesses working in their plots that had just seen me making a complete fool of myself! Then there was the time I had my first practice at using my 'She-wee', when my shed doors refused to stay closed in the wind, leaving me with no privacy. The only screen to hand was a large cardboard box, which acted like a saloon door and just about covered the essential areas. It was a race against time to finish my business, before the combine harvester got within viewing range in the field next door. Imagine my luck, when on top of all this, a wasp decided to raid the shed whilst I am in mid-flow! Having an allotment is not always a delight, but memories are certainly made!

It has been nice to share new information I find with the other plot holders, such as joining the NAS; The National Allotment Society. It was relatively cheap to join and the perks are brilliant.

They give all their members free allotment insurance as well as offering super discounts with their recommended suppliers. This was beneficial when it came to ordering the seeds for next year.

In return, the other allotment holders have shared valuable information with me. It was lovely to see some drone photos that one lady had taken, it showed all my hard efforts and I could compare it to the empty plot on the previous years photo.

As well as information and seedlings, we have shared all manner of materials. There is the gentleman who delivers the manure for us all and a kind man in the local village who drops of free wood chippings. I have often been seen putting my read magazines into the storage bench for a lady a few plots away. Our little Jack Russell Oreo has also been seen having playdates with the other dogs on site as it seems the whole family benefits from the allotment community.

D is for Disease and Pests

As previously mentioned, growing Veg is not for the faint hearted. There are some that grow with just a bit of muck and the odd water, like Potatoes and Radishes but then even these have their nemeses. Each and every plant seems to have its own battle to win in order to grow to its full potential. Never would I have thought that plants can have mould or swellings!

Within the first few months of having our plot, we had been unfortunate enough to discover Powdery Mildew, Brown Leaf Spot, Blossom End Rot and Root Rot. The Powdery Mildew was probably the strangest, as in a single weekend all the foliage on the Courgettes and Pumpkins had turned a dusty white. I would love to liken it to a snowy covering, but it had more the look of a mouldy loaf of bread found a month past its Use By date. It seems that Powdery Mildew is in fact quite common and is air born, so likely came from another source nearby. Once again, I entrusted the advice from the fellow plot holders and removed all the effected foliage and chucked them in the garden waste bin at home (I certainly wasn't about to risk adding them to the compost and doubling the problem). I was reassured that the mildew does not affect the fruit, but just slows down the production of them.

As disgusting as it sounds, Blossom End Rot is when the tips of the fruit decide to turn all yucky and brown. I found this one out after bragging about my amazing crop of Courgettes and how I would share them out with all the football mums the following week. How disappointed was I when I went to pick a few and they were like a wet sponge. Not much could be done for the poor Courgette plant, as I later found out I had planted them all far too close and the air could not circulate properly.

Halfway through the season, I discovered a couple of websites that can help prepare for the onslaught on some diseases, such as Blight. Blight is a fungal-like organism that spreads rapidly in wet weather, causing the decay of tomatoes and potatoes. The website allowed me to register for Blight updates when the disease was rife in the local area.

To my horror our Potatoes which were doing so well suddenly began to wilt and the foliage died back. I tried for a long while to discover which disease they were suffering from, but to no avail. I was after seeking advice from a neighbouring plot holder that we learnt the foliage does die back when the potatoes are in fact ready to harvest and were not dying at all. Clearly I stood out as a total novice gardener at this point, but everyone has to start somewhere.

Disease and Viruses are not the only battle the poor plants have, they also face pests. Right from the very beginning, we decided we wanted to encourage wildlife and would therefore use Organic Gardening methods, which is super for the environment but a challenge for novice gardeners.

When the Broccoli and Radishes became home to a thousand and one flea beetles, I desperately wanted to save them with the power of synthetic pesticides: quick and easy. I just could not undo all our hard work in encouraging the insects, by spraying them and killing them. Instead, we googled the best remedy and used soapy water instead.

Our Gooseberry bush was bare of fruit thanks to Harry doing a thorough job harvesting them. But what I did not know about was the Sawfly. Within a week, all the foliage on our gooseberry bush had been eaten and it looked like we had just planted a few spikey sticks. For future situations, we now have the trusted soap and water which will get rid of any unwanted sawfly larvae that appear.

Another of the famous pests we encountered, was the black fly. I first spotted their arrival when checking the beans and noticing a few frothy looking white eggs. Without hesitation, I wiped these off the bean stalks and disposed of them into the bin. This seemed to do the job, and we did not have any further experiences this summer with black flies.

I decided to join an online Organic Gardening Course to learn about environmentally friendly methods of Gardening, including the use of pesticides and fertilisers. It took me a good few months, but I passed with 97% and a Distinction. I should have little excuse now and can help my children learn more about Organic methods also.

Having learnt about netting with the Brassicas, I decided to bulk buy a roll and use it on almost everything; prevention is better than cure! As we were setting up our allotment during a period of Covid Lockdown, my work as a Wedding Photographer was in hibernation and we had little disposable income to spend on luxuries like fruit cages and covers. This meant being creative and making whatever we could from wherever we can. I was keen to teach the children about 'Mending and Making do', and what better time to promote this ethos. We used any freebies that were kindly offered to gather enough materials to convert into useful items for the allotment. We made some super vegetable bed covers from wooden shelving, netting and a staple gun.

As previously mentioned, the Brassicas should definitely be covered all year round from those pesky Cabbage White Butterflies. The fine netting also deters slugs, snails and other insects that can cause damage to the plants. The larger netting can be used for any plant subject to the likes of Hedgehogs, Birds, Rodents, and such like, although it needs to be pegged down and secured with strong methods. However, creatures like foxes and rabbits can break through most barriers when they are determined and hungry.

I saw on a programme that adding ladybirds to the garden can be beneficial in reducing the number of pests, as they eat Aphids and Blackflies. There is in fact places that farm ladybirds and enable you to purchase them in bulk, but I thought I would multi-task and buy the children a Ladybird mini farm for Christmas. This consists of a plastic container with instructions on how to raise and release ladybirds. As well as educating the children, I can use them on the allotment when it comes time for the release.

Having mentioned quite a few of the diseases and pests we have incurred so far, I have failed to mention the worst culprit of all, the children! It came to the point where I erected a 'make do' fruit cage from netting offcuts and pallet wood, to keep the Strawberries and Gooseberries safe from the boys! My husband asked if we were actually growing any fruit and when would I be bringing some home, because the majority got eaten on site and never made it further than the allotment gate.

The funniest learning curve from these 3 human pests, was when I asked Harry to harvest the Gooseberries for me. For some reason, I assumed he would know to only pick the large and ripe Gooseberries, not strip the entire bush of any sign of fruit whatsoever! We had Gooseberry Jam for weeks after and he has since been banned from the fruit cage!

E is for Experiments

The local freebie site has given us so many bargains, like the car full of bricks I picked up to make our Herb Spiral and the pallets that we made the fruit cage from. We have also experimented with things like an old dog kennel, making it into a Hedgehog House for the communal plots and a large circular planter that we turned into a sunken pond. We love to create as much as we can from freebies and items that would otherwise be taken to the dumps.

I think the most striking item we made using freebies is the Bean Den. It consists of a pallet for the base, and 2 cot sides tied together to make an A frame over the pallet. We grew French Beans up it this year, which the children loved. They could sit inside the den and have a picnic, then pick beans from above their heads.

The pallets have been dismantled and used for so many things, but a few we left whole and used as planters. The Tomatoes and Peppers grow extremely well in soil which we embedded between the pallet planks. I think that the wooden edges of the pallet helped support the tomatoes in all the strong winds we have. In the Autumn, once the tomato plants had been pulled, we sowed the Onions sets into the pallets instead. I hope that the onions have enough space to fully develop, but only time will tell.

Some of the dismantled pallet wood helped me to build a bench from a wooden bed. I used the headboard as the back of the bench and the foot board as the front. Using the pallet wood, I was able

 to connect the front and back and make the slatted part to sit on. The children helped me paint it yellow and it now has pride of place in the allotment. Harry really enjoyed using the crowbar to dismantle the pallets and Alfie helped George to drill the screws in. It was a team effort to create our bench and we are all enormously proud.

Most of the plants this year have also been experiments, from not knowing what they were, to learning how to care for them and finally cook them. As a family, we have enjoyed new meals with the Butternut Celebration Squash, yellow Courgettes and Purple Cauliflowers, all items we would never normally buy from the supermarket. The major lesson we learnt with the Courgettes, is that one plant is enough to feed a family for several weeks. After we were given 3 Courgette seedlings and planted them all, we had enough Courgettes to feed several families for a few months!

Having been given a lot of our first year's plants, we just went along with it and planted them all. When we were offered some Sweet Bell Pepper seedlings, we kindly accepted them knowing that we would get more use from them. What we did not envisage, was a bag of over 50 seedlings that the lady had cultivated from her own peppers earlier in the year. Again, taught not to waste, with the help from the children we sowed all 50 of the seedlings and watched every single one grow. Even now, almost 3 months later, I am still offering Bell Pepper plants to anyone that will take one!

The Pumpkins were quite an experiment too. There were 3 plants left at the garden centre, which I quickly snapped up. We had left it a bit late in the season to plant pumpkin seeds, but the children desperately wanted to grow some but due to some  greenhouse, slug and sunburn issues we lost all 3 of these plants.

The children were disheartened, so I decided it was worth an attempt at growing our own as we had nothing to lose. Alfie sowed 12 pumpkin seeds that we were given and he nurtured them carefully. Only five of these germinated, but five is better than none.

After a few weeks the weather was warm enough and the pumpkin seedlings strong enough for us to plant out into an empty bed we had made. We were warned that pumpkin vines grow big, but we did not appreciate how big. They were soon creeping their way out of the bed and across the surrounding pathways. I was the first to come to a muddy end when I tripped and went skidding across the adjacent newly manured bed. At the time, I was mortified, but the children found it highly amusing.

Out of the 5 plants, all of which succumbed to powdery mildew, we managed to harvest 6 beautiful Pumpkins. They varied in sizes, one was a perfect round tennis ball shape and went bright orange very quickly. The others were more cylindrical and only 3 of them turned a full orange. I think because we planted them so late in the season, they did not have quite enough sunlight in the day to allow them to turn completely orange. But nonetheless, the children carved some super faces at Halloween and we enjoyed some yummy cupcakes from the flesh inside.

One of the most productive experiments we have undertaken is the paths. Unbeknown to us, the areas surrounding the plots and the actual plots themselves are prone to light flooding in heavy rain. This is due to the clay soil; the same soil I was praising in the heat of the Summer for retaining the moisture. Even wearing wellies, the clay sticks to your soles and leaves a footprint filled with water behind. On our plot, we have created lots of smaller vegetable beds and a flower garden at the front, meaning there are a lot of pathways between the beds. As these turned to a boggy mess in the rain, it was essential we laid down a firmer substance for walking on. Having looked at the other plots on the site, it seems that cardboard with bark chippings on top is the preferred method of creating a walkable path. Going by this, we got to work and laid meters of heavy card down and covered it with wood chip from a local tree surgeon. Hopefully, this will see us through a couple of Winters and can easily be replaced. Time will tell if it also suppresses the weeds, but fingers crossed it does!

Along one edge of the path, we have laid down some guttering that we were given during a friend's house renovation. The boys filled the gutters with compost and soil, then sprinkled a mixture of wildflower seeds inside. We are hoping that in the Spring there will be a beautiful array of flowers welcoming us down the path.

It will be nice next year to see all the beautiful flowers bloom and we hope that our willow cuttings will have sprouted by then too. One of the ladies a few plots away gave us a handful of foot high willow cuttings, which having learnt how quickly they can spread and how far their roots can grow, we potted them into a long trough style planter. Hopefully, when they mature a little, the trough will sit nicely behind the bean den and enclose the back with greenery for the children.

I spent a lot of the summer learning about propagating and how to save money by growing my own plants from ones I already have. I was successful in getting many of the cuttings to take root and in fact had so many I shared them with friends and family. I grew quite a few passion flowers, Lemon Verbenas, Basil, Mints and Lavender. Some of the Passion Flower we have planted up a metal arch in the Allotment and I hope next year it will look absolutely beautiful and visible from the entire site.

I think that is the fun of the allotment, all the experimenting and the adrenaline rush when it all works out. We have learnt so many lessons through experimenting and I do not think this will ever stop even as we become more established gardeners.

F is for Fertilisers

I can't be the only person to have driven past bags of Manure for sale and wondered who on earth would want to buy a bag full of poo, and even worse, who would want to shovel it into a bag to sell in the first place. Now though, I find myself checking the prices as I drive past!

When we first got our allotment, the man in the plot next door said that the most important part of growing veg is the soil. He claimed he had spent months digging down 4ft and mixing well rotted manure, compost, and such like into his soil. At this point came the onset of panic, no way was I prepared to do that and I am quite certain my back would not allow me to do that either. Luckily, whilst reading one of the many Gardening Magazines I seem to have rounded up I came across an article about the 'No Dig' method. It made absolute sense, and with the newfound knowledge that digging the soil could cause more harm than good due to disrupting the natural soil structure I was sold.

The allotment already had a compost bin when we arrived, and I was kindly gifted another soon after. So, with two Dalek looking compost bins waiting to be filled I had no excuses. Simply by adding well-rotted manure, compost, shredded paper and soil on top of the grass I could instantly make some ready to go vegetable beds. There was no need to dig, no need to go out and purchase a lot of topsoil etc. and even better, we could get planting right away. The compost bin was half full when we arrived, so I could use that compost straight away and re-fill it instead of using the garden waste bin at home.

Since we have started growing the veg, we have noticed the difference between those which have a good supply of fertiliser in the soil and those which have not, such as the containers. The Leeks really like to be in manure rich soil and the Courgettes quite liked the shredded paper mulch we gave them. The tomatoes seem to prefer a liquid feed solution, which when mixed with water supplies them with a boost of micro-nutrients.

As well as liquid feeds we discovered that we should occasionally give the plants a dose of organic based general-purpose plant food such as Blood, Fish and Bone. This gives the plants a quick boost and encourages flowering, so an all-round good fertiliser. Be warned though that it does smell rather pungent and looks like a jug of year-old gravy when mixed up!

For centuries, people have used Seaweed to replenish the soil. It is full of macro and micronutrients that plants need, as well as vitamins, amino acids and more. The combination of these and other active ingredients has been proven to enhance plant growth by prolonging the Chlorophyll which aids photosynthesis.

Using Seaweed Tea (pre-rinsed Seaweed and water) every 7-10 days during certain periods of plant growth can be a cheap and easy way to benefit your crops. You only need a small amount of seaweed, 20ml to 5l of water. This will help the plants produce more and bigger fruits.

Collecting more than 20 litres of seaweed from beaches requires a permit but a small amount is allowed for personal use within habitat protection zones and general use zones. I managed to get a small amount of Fucus Serratus Seaweed, which I rinsed and added to a garden bin of water and left it to ferment over Winter. But it smells horrendous so I have left the lid slightly off to allow air circulation. This should be more than enough to see me through the next year of growth.

One thing that I have often wondered is what people do with all the fallen leaves that smother their driveways in Autumn. I have seen bags of leaves squirreled away in friends' gardens before, but never had the need to ask why. It wasn't until we were given a sack full of leaves by a neighbour that I found out what to do with them. Although it takes a couple of years, Leaf Compost is supposed to be the most amazing thing for the garden and much better than chemical fertilisers. It nourishes plants, preserves moisture in the ground, suppresses weeds and encourages the arrival of worms. Now we have our very own sack of leaves squirreled away in the corner of our allotment, ready for use in a few years.

The most natural soil aid that we have found is the worms, they are simply amazing. I did not realise they do such an important job and the kids enjoy discovering them in every patch of soil. I have been looking into setting up a Worm Composter, which involves farming worms and feeding them our food scraps. In return we use the worm castings for fertiliser and the worm urine, known as 'golden liquid', to mix into a plant feed. These are very costly, so will be something we perhaps purchase next year, but I am sure the children would love to have some pet worms.

My husband found it rather odd that one day, the postman delivered us an envelope labelled 'Livestock'. He was even more shocked at how excited I was to receive this envelope and the look on his face was priceless when he realised it was a bag full of Tiger Worms. I had read in a brochure that adding worms to the compost pile can speed up the process and enhance the result with their urine and castings.

On our sites' communal plot there is a pile of manure that one man helpfully keeps topped up. We all have access to use this manure and I have done so on several occasions. However, a little word of advice, it is always worth checking how long the pile has been there before using it. Thank goodness it was me and not the children, who dug up a very shiny animal skull when barrowing the manure to the plot. I was horrified but much to my surprise, the children thought it was fantastic and chose to display it pride of place on the garden table! At first glance I thought it was a rat's skull but I have since been assured (although saddened of course) that is a rabbit skull. I have no idea how it got there but it must have been there a while to become so clean and decay-free. Lesson learnt here, always wear gloves!

One day when we were re-potting some plants, Alfie found a bean that I must have dropped. Assuming it was a magic Bean and would grow into a colossal beanstalk harbouring a real Giant at the top, he asked to plant it. Any mummy would assumingly give the same answer at his thrilled little face, "Of course you can". Off Alfie went and planted his seed as deep as he could, somewhere that it would grow perfectly, in the 70-litre bag of compost. Now it is the waiting game to see which plants and whereabouts in the allotment that the compost containing the magic bean has been used. I am sure it will not be long until a casual beanstalk appears somewhere unexpectedly and brightens Alfie's day once again. Lesson learnt, always listen intently to your children and ensure they follow exacting instructions.

G is for Greenhouse

I can only really start this chapter off by telling you about the five greenhouses I have gone through, yes five, in five months! Desperate to grow Cucumbers and to start the Pumpkins seedlings off in a warmer climate, I knew I had to have a greenhouse.

So, the journey of Greenhouses began with a small 3-tiered, metal pole frame and plastic cover that I picked up for £7. We are not allowed glass on the site, so all these Greenhouses were made of a metal frame and plastic covers. I quickly found that the 3 tiers were not anywhere near big enough for my ambitious plans and so next one was a 5 tier. However, these both came to an unsettling end during high winds. Coming down to the plot to discover a heap of poles, plastic and pots was not a nice experience but somehow the cucumber seedlings survived and lived to give me a huge harvest.

So not having learnt my lesson and never one to quit, I purchased a large walk-in greenhouse for a minimal amount second hand. This was the one, I loved it! It was big enough to house everything and keep me dry from the rain too, bonus! I made sure I put heavy slabs on the bottom poles and tied it to my shed with gardening string. I thought it was bombproof, but again it could not stand up to the wind that blows ferociously from the fields and across the allotments. There was no saving it, the covers were torn, the poles were bent, and the connectors were snapped. Thankfully though I did manage to rescue the cucumbers again and brought them home for safe keeping.

The fourth greenhouse was kindly bought for me by my Nanny

and it was a lot sturdier, having a wooden frame. The cover however is still plastic but I secured it to the frame with wood screws. So far it has withstood the weather and has been home to seedlings of all types, including Broad Beans, Peas, Cauliflowers, Sweet Pea, Violas, Velvet poppies and more.

My nanny was kind enough to pass on her favourite gardening books to me. One of the books was an older edition, all about greenhouse gardening. It was intriguing to read about all the varieties of plants which can be grown in the greenhouse and especially the ones which can flourish over winter. The most interesting part of the book for me though, was that all the pricing was in old money. Seeing that a greenhouse used to cost around £15, which converts into around £900 in new money. Seeds were sold in shillings and thruppence, units of currency that I never got to experience.

You may have already discovered, that when it comes to Seed Catalogues and ordering, the heart rate can easily raise and the fingers can get what I call 'click happy'. This happened to me and I ended up with a huge order including Baby Watermelons, Luffas and Crystal Cucumbers. It did not cross my mind at the time of ordering that these in fact grow rather large on vines and all require the heat of a greenhouse. At this point it would be cheaper and easier to just return, sell or ignore those seeds but it would be such a shame after all the excitement they have brought me. Hence greenhouse No 5, a plastic square with no shelves, perfect for growing vines! Having already learnt that Mother Nature is obviously a lot stronger and smarter than me I have built this greenhouse a wooden frame from old pallets in the hope to give it more stability. I guess after the upcoming Winter, we are going to be able to tell if my frame withstood the weather.

To keep our plants warm I decided it would be beneficial to get a Cold frame. These are commonly a rectangular frame with glass or polycarbonate that keep plants warm during frosts and can also help to climatise plants coming from the inside to outdoors.

These are not the cheapest and being without work because of Covid, I am very aware of having to make do with items that are found free or extremely cheap. This is how the Cold Frame Cabinet came to life. On the local freebie site a lady was advertising a wooden ottoman which had seen better days. It was perfect for a cold frame after I stripped it down of all its upholstery, covered the lid in a thick clear PVC material and painted it with a yellow wood stain. It has a hinged lid so I can leave it open to allow air to the plants but close it on chillier days and allow the sun to penetrate the PVC window in the lid.

I really want the loofa plant to grow well and these require the warmth of a greenhouse. I have seen them planted out in warmer weather successfully, but our summers are so short that they would do a lot better kept inside. I thought that loofa's were made from some sort of sea plant, but that could not be farther from the truth. Loofa's are grown on tall vines and when the fruit is left to dry, it leaves behind a sort of skeleton looking sponge. This is the loofa sponge that many of us use in the bath and the result that I would love to achieve.

I have concluded that a greenhouse is essential for growing the less hardy plants and for those who wish to stretch the UK growing limits a little further. With the seeds at the ready we cannot wait for Spring, to start growing our more exotic plants.

H is for Harvest Time

The Harvest is the time we look forward to the most, although the children have been harvesting the tomatoes and berries on a weekly basis. Due to getting our allotment late in the year we have been growing the seedlings that we were given and not those we would necessarily have chosen ourselves. This means that the harvesting times have all been a surprise and quite sporadic.

The Strawberries were growing in abundance when we arrived and besides consolidating the majority into one bed, we left them the do their own thing. It was not long before we had a huge array of fresh Strawberries to enjoy and I am not entirely sure many even made it home.

The Raspberries that were already growing in the corner of the plot have also provided us with weekly snacks. There seems to be a good mixture of Summer and Autumn varieties, meaning a continuous supply for a few months.

The largest harvest we have had is from all the Tomato plants we were given with a range of plum, beef and cherry types. Again, a lot of these were eaten straight from the vines but the vast majority did make it home and we had some lovely meals from them. Towards the end of the Summer the tomatoes were not ripening as well as before, and our neighbouring plot holders advised us to remove some of the foliage and allow the light to get to them better. We also gave them a dose of high potash plant food which helped a little. In the end though, we cultivated the whole lot and bought them home to ripen as the wet weather would soon cause them to rot and become bird food.

I think we could have survived on Courgettes and Squash alone this year with several Courgettes plants and four squash plants, we have an absolute abundance of them. The Courgettes were yellow and tasted extremely sweet. We used them with  rice, casseroles, chicken and pasta dishes too. The squashes were a mix of Kuri and Celebration and were used in our curries and as mash.

Whilst trying to pass our glut of Courgettes to any willing takers, I found out that a Marrow is in fact just an overgrown Courgette. I always thought they were two different varieties of vegetable!

The children enjoyed picking the Peas and Beans and would bring me a handful most times we visited the plot. It was fun teaching them how to pop the peas from their pods and use the tools to create the green beans for our roast dinner. I did have to stop a pea fight breaking out one evening when they realised you could squeeze the pea pod and shoot peas at quite a distance. I am planning on growing a lot more beans and peas next season, as we enjoyed them so much.

Every allotment needs a crop of the staple carrots and potatoes. We managed to grow just one singular carrot, which the children found quite amusing. It had a beautiful green top and looked huge but when we pulled it up the laughter erupted at our extremely short and stumpy lonesome carrot. The potatoes were a better result and we all thoroughly enjoyed tipping the sacks into the barrows and hunting down the hidden spuds. It was surprising how many grew from just planting two old, wrinkly potatoes.

They were delicious served with butter and seasoning and we will certainly be growing more. In fact, Alfie has planted some Maris Pipers which will hopefully be ready in time for Christmas dinner.

The good thing about growing potatoes is that they can be grown through most of the year and even if you harvest them too early, they can still be used. We harvested some too early and they were a lot smaller than anticipated but they were perfect for adding to a casserole without the need to peel and dice them.

One of the easiest crops we have grown so far are the Radishes. We simply put the seeds in the soil and within a few weeks we had radishes! The Black Spanish ones were extremely hot and we gave them away, but the pink ones we really liked. In total we grew four batches of Radishes and could have eaten more had the weather allowed.

When we harvested our Sweetcorn, we did not realise that the bottom 4 cobs had not been pollinated. They looked full and ripe from the outside but the kernels inside were shrivelled and pale. We had enjoyed the cobs previously harvested, so we decided we could afford to share these ones with the birds. We took them home and hung them on our bird table; it was a delight watching them provide good meals to a vast array of birds.

As mentioned in previous chapters, the Cucumbers will definitely be grown again, but this time we will grow them correctly to ensure a good harvest. The fun in harvesting is also deciding how to consume the food and what new recipes can we use. I only have to put a request for suggestions on social media and the ideas come flooding in. I never thought that Courgettes could be used in so many ways, including cakes and biscuits!

I is for Improvement

When beginning with an area of grass and weeds, it is quite easy to make any small improvement but an overall improvement for me would benefit both the local wildlife and the biodiversity of the area. The children cemented my idea of making the allotment as valuable for the animals and insects as well as for ourselves, making both habitats and produce.

If communities do not make use of the allotments, they will be lost and forgotten and eventually become additional concrete buildings which the world already has plenty of. So, we took the bull by the horns and began cultivating the land almost immediately. There were already some fruits growing, which we chose to keep and eventually multiply and we started by growing some tomatoes. After the initial plants  were sown we aimed to add to the plot as often as possible. It was within just 4 months that the whole plot was re-designed, and we had over twenty different foods growing.

We kept an area at the front to grow flowers to encourage the pollinators and added a small pond for an extra little habitat. Our friends, family and the neighbouring plot holders were impressed with how quickly we managed to improve the plot and in such a diverse way.

It is quite easy to improve areas with planting and cultivation. By simply growing plants, you are improving the air quality. The plants absorb the Carbon Dioxide and release Oxygen. This in turn will improve your health and the areas around you. I know plants have a positive effect on your Serotonin levels and I certainly feel less stressed when I'm at the allotment.

It is very uplifting for both the children and I to see the different habitats we have created being appreciated by all sorts of species, from insects through to birds and Hedgehogs. The biodiversity found in the allotment shows that the huge variety of plants we are growing, particularly the larger plants support so much wildlife. They provide food, nesting sites, cover and much more.

Our efforts have certainly improved our plot but they have also improved our diets. We have no excuse any more to avoid eating our five-a-day. With the abundance of fruits and vegetables at our fingertips, we have never eaten so healthily. The children now ask to try the different foods we have grown and have ideas about what to grow in future. Their knowledge of nutrition has certainly improved and my knowledge of gardening has also.

My husband has commented on the improvement to our bank balance since growing our own food. Quite often organic produce in supermarkets is at a premium price and out of our budget. But now, we can enjoy almost unlimited organic fruit and vegetables throughout the year for free. Our family and friends also benefit when we have glut, as seen with the courgettes and tomatoes.

I would also like to add that my physique has seen an improvement. The physical effort that an allotment requires to setup is demanding and somewhat impressive. I have received comments about my muscular looking thighs and toned upper arms. Considering I am on the larger side of the gene pool and am awaiting double knee surgery, this has left me feeling rather good and spurred me on to do more.

J is for Journal

It is so uplifting to look back on a gloomy day and see the progress that has been made on our Allotment. Not only does it make a huge positive impact on our lifestyle, but it is great for our mindfulness and has had a small but beneficial impact on the regeneration of the Earth.

When we began in June 2020, we were working with a six metre by seventeen metre patch of grass, mainly covered in weeds. It has taken us less than five months to turn this patch around and achieve an abundance of produce from it. Although hard work at first, it has certainly paid off.

Not only can we see the progress through the photo evidence, but by recording the amount of produce we grew and comparing to the supermarket prices we can see a huge £200 saving in just five months. We did not set out to create our allotment to save money, but it has certainly been a benefit, especially as earnings have been low due to the Covid 19 Lockdown.

When we plant news seeds we like to take a couple of photos every few weeks to visually compare how much they have grown. The children are always amazed at how a tiny seed can produce a plant and how quickly too. The thought that one Pumpkin seed has led to thousands more being formed is incredible and it strengthens the fact that it is possible to solely live off the land.

When we look back over our photos it is hard to believe what we have achieved with just a small plot of land. We had no gardening experience whatsoever when we began, but our photograph and our mental journal have shown how easy it is to learn and achieve in a short space of time. During Lockdown many of us parents were suddenly thrown into the realm of teaching. I absolutely love being a Mummy, but I never thought I would become the children's teacher too. The Allotment has given me the chance to teach the children through outdoor play. It has in fact made Lockdown a lot easier in that we could spend hours gardening and growing, without the boys realising that they were learning at the same time. The struggle of sitting them down with a pen and paper was almost obsolete and we could email photos into school to document their learning.

It will be interesting to grow new crops next Spring and compare them to those we grew this year. Perhaps having learnt how to prepare and rejuvenate our soil over Winter will make a difference to the new plant's growth potential. Maybe the new raise beds will have a different requirement when it comes to moisture retention and the rotation of the crops could be affected by the wind or shade.

By recording our progress in photos and on our social media page 'Allotment – Learn, Mend and Make Do', we can also keep the fun memories alive. The faces made when the boys first shoveled manure, the expressions when they dug up their first potatoes and the sheer amusement when we popped all the peas from their pods. These memories will last us a lifetime and I hope that when I am long gone from this Earth my future generations can look back over our story and it may inspire them to become more in tune with nature and grow their own food too.

K is for Kitchen Gardening

Since I was little I have often had a dabble in the kitchen, going through stages of trying new recipes and then getting stuck in a rut. Having had an abundance of foods from the allotment this year I have been nudged into finding new and exciting recipes to incorporate them all.

I have tried to encourage the children to eat the rainbow since they were tiny and the allotment is doing wonders in promoting all the rainbow coloured vegetables and fruit available. The red coloured is good for a strong heart, orange helps us to see in the dark, yellow assists cuts to heal faster, green fights sickness, blue aids a strong brain and white gives us energy.

With all the delicious yellow Courgettes making an appearance in August, I do not think there is a recipe we have not unearthed that does not include them. The children have hinted that they are absolutely fed up with having Courgettes in most of their meals! I managed to hide them in Bolognese, Lasagna, Jambalaya and even cakes. We did enjoy the meals but there is such a thing as too many Courgettes.

This is where I have learnt that growing to cater for the needs of the family is important. This year we grew every plant we were offered, but next year we have a plan to suit us. Lots of magazines include free packets of seeds, the majority of which seem to be lettuce and kale. Although we do eat these, we do not have a huge requirement for them leaving us with a tub full of spare seeds. The local freebie page has been offered some and fellow Allotmenteers too.

We sporadically sowed some beetroot seeds one morning but in our haste the packet tore and a great quantity of seeds flew into the soil in a heap. Knowing through my nannies cooking that beetroots grow rather large I also knew that they must require a fair bit of space between seedlings. As the seeds were so tiny there was not much we could do to rectify the spillage, so we raked the soil a bit and left them to grow.

Much to our delight, we soon saw lots of tiny purple seedlings growing through and it was immediately apparent these were far too close together. The root systems of beetroots are fragile and do not cope well with disruption, so the prospect of thinning them and moving them about was not a viable option. It didn't matter though, as we were not relying on the crop for anything other than an additional ingredient in the kitchen.

After a couple of months, there were some reasonable looking beetroots poking through the soil and we decided to harvest them. Although small, they were perfectly formed and the majority were the equivalent size to a tennis ball. I found a lovely sounding recipe which involved dicing them and coating them in herbs and spices, before roasting them in the oven. Needless to say, they went down well and we all really enjoyed them.

One plant I do hope to grow next year is Quinoa, as it is exceptionally good for us and can be added to a huge variety of meals. I ordered some seeds online hoping to grow in a 2m x 1m bed. When the seeds arrived however I had **nine** packets with about a million seeds in each. These have also been offered out as I do not fancy a glut of Quinoa come the Summer and simply do not have the space to grow them all.

It is tempting to grow everything we are offered but with limited space we must make strict decisions. With planning the layout for plants next year it is possible for crops to fill gaps and to replace those plants that are harvested early in the year. For instance, as Radishes grow quickly and are small I can plant these in between other crops like the Cauliflower. The Garlic that is growing over Winter can be harvested early Summer, so it can make room for late sowings of Potatoes.

At present, we have approximately 20 leeks trying to grow. The reason I say trying, is because they do not seem to have grown much since we planted them as seedlings a month ago. I have been reassured that they can be left in the ground over winter to mature and I will be able to enjoy my favourite leek and potato soup after Christmas.

The fruit in the allotment very rarely makes it home to the kitchen as the boys eat it straight from the plant. After speaking to my nanny, she has given me a mature apple tree to plant in the Allotment. It has been in a pot in her garden and provided her with several bumper crops for a few years but she now has two apple trees and only requires one. I am hoping the apples make it home as the children may not be able to reach to the top.

There are other fruit trees I would love to grow but do not have the room such as plum and pear. It would also be great to grow Rhubarb as I have seen some recipes for rhubarb jam I would like to try. Unfortunately, though, Rhubarb takes up a lot of space and there are more useful Vegetables we would like to produce.

Using our crops to create meals is really rewarding and the sense of pride the children have is really encouraging. In fact, they were disappointed when we used up the supply of sweetcorn from the allotment and had to resort back to store bought. We could all taste the significant difference in flavour from home grown to store bought.

L is for Low Maintenance

During the initial Lockdown we had so much time on our hands to tend to the Allotment. It was great because we had to start from scratch and begin the journey from a blank canvas. However, now the boys are back to school and the weather is not quite so pleasant time on the allotment is reduced. Making the plot as low maintenance, whilst providing the highest yield is especially important to us.

There are a few ways in which we have managed to do this so far, as finding the perfect balance takes time and experience. My photography work has been on the back burner since the Prime Minister keeps locking down the hospitality industry, so I have a lot of hours during the week to spend at the Allotment. This is convenient for me but means the children miss out on a lot of the fun and interesting jobs. They are disappointed when I have harvested food without them or sown new seeds.

Over the last month, since they have been back to school, I have been getting on with the less gracious side of gardening such as shoveling the manure and rotating the compost heaps. It is important to look after the soil as it is the key ingredient to growing healthy plants. To make life easier in the Spring when the busy planting period arrives, I have been basing my days' work on the soil preparation.

The soil loses a lot of its key nutrients to the plants each year so these need replenishing over the Winter. I have found the easiest way to do this is to add a mix of shredded paper, well-rotted horse manure, compost, leaf mulch, grass clippings and topsoil to the beds. Slowly over the wetter months, the worms and microorganisms help to rot down the added ingredients and create a super healthy and rich soil, ready for the new plants. A spare plot on site is always being topped up with Manure, and I gather up the grass clippings throughout the year. Although these come free and are easily accessible for us, you can pick these up free or cheaply in most areas.

This year, I quickly learnt that even though I added all these wonderful elements into the soil, it does not stop the weeds from continuing to sprout. Luckily, the other plot holders were keen to advise me to cover the beds up with a permeable weed membrane until I am ready to use them again in Spring. This prevents the sunlight from aiding the growth of weeds, and the materials underneath are left undisturbed.

As well as low maintenance preventative actions, we found out it is also important to have some quick and easy remedies to hand for those unexpected instances. This is referring to the pests we had visit our plot, like the Flea Beetles and Aphids. We now keep a spray bottle of water mixed with soap, which we can quickly use to deter them if the pests should appear again. I also save all the eggshells we use, and once crushed I scatter them at the base of vulnerable plants. The slugs and snails do not like moving across the sharp shells and it prevents a lot of damage being caused.

I am hoping that laying down some paths will help keep the maintenance of the weeds and grass down next year. I seemed to spend a lot of time pulling up unwanted weeds and keeping the grass cut this year, which took away from time tending to the plants. To lay the paths, we simply put a thick layer of cardboard down between the beds and covered it in bark chippings. This will hopefully last us a couple of years and can easily be replaced as and when necessary.

With weeds, it is almost impossible to prevent them from growing in a bed full of plants. I have been told that by adding a layer of mulch around the plants it can help suppress the weeds by limiting the sunlight that reaches them. I am going to give this a try, anything to reduce those annoying weeds. The less time we spend maintaining the plot, the more time we have to enjoy it.

I have discovered that growing a ground covering plant such as Nasturtiums can help reduce weeds as it denies the weeds access to light and consumes the bulk of the nutrients available in the soil. Nasturtiums are also great for pest control, as they attract the Aphids away from the crops. But even better is that the flowers and leaves of the nasturtiums are edible, adding a peppery taste to salads and a sweetness to cakes.

As it is fairly quiet with essential jobs to do during the Autumn, I think I will spend a couple of days tidying up and cleaning the tools in our shed. The secateurs and Hoes could do with being sharpened and treated against rust. The pots need to also be cleaned, to prevent the spread of any fungus or diseases that may be harboring in them. If I do these little but essential tasks now, it will save an onslaught of jobs to do in the Springtime.

Keeping on top of things is probably the easiest way to conserve time and effort. We keep all our seeds in a container, in order of when they need to be sown. I also devised a month-by-month chart, which hangs on our fridge alongside a plan of the Allotment. It was suggested to us that by making a plan of the Allotment, demonstrating where we want to grow each crop, will help us minimise the mistakes and overspending on seeds etc. Anything advice to help save the pennies is greatly appreciated.

M is for Mental Health

I have been reading a lot lately about the healing Power of gardening. It amazes me how only a small percent of the GPs in the UK recommends gardening as a form of medicine for the mind. I wish it had been suggested for me to do some gardening when I developed Post Natal Depression and had to depend on Anti-Depressants to see me through an emotional period. It has been proven for many years that gardening helps reduce stress, anxiety and is great exercise at the same time. Some areas on the UK prescribe time on a communal garden/allotment to help patients.

Scientists have discovered that a micro-bacterium in the soil can improve the brains function and boost moods. This is because the micro-bacterium increases the levels of serotonin produced in the brain. The experts have also proven that something as simple as a plant on your desk can significantly improve the way you feel, reduce stress, and fell more energized.

We have had many laughs on the plot and made some wonderful memories, from having digging races to enjoying family picnics. I even made a little hopscotch from paving slabs and it brightens our mood every we time we use it. The children squeal with joy whilst creating masterpieces in their pallet wood mud kitchen. Being knee deep in muck and as far away from technology as possible, they thrive in the natural environment.

Since getting our allotment, I have found my mood is a lot better on days I have tended to the allotment. It has given me focus and drive, it provides ambition and accomplishment, it has helped my physical ability and bonded the family with memory making. Our youngest son who has ADHD and Autism has hugely benefited from being at the allotment. Not being restricted to a certain schedule of learning and being free to explore and learn at his own leisure has been valuable for his mental health too. We have seen him keen to discover and get involved with the plants, the creatures and even develop his social skills with the other children on the site. A price cannot be put in the wellbeing of a child and I can only wish that outdoor learning becomes a more integral part of the UK education system.

I can see through my own eyes and my children's, just how much a small space of earth can make such a difference. Did you know, in World War 1, the soldiers would dig allotments and gardens into the trenches to help them deal with their emotions. It gave them time to forget about the horrific effects of war.

Having a garden or allotment is also a great conversation topic, it neither divides nor isolates people. There is always something to discuss and relate to when considering the beauty of nature herself. We have made friends, shared advice, and even shared our harvests. There is a real sense of community and belonging on our site.

It is also great to see the Royal Family and the Media pushing the link between mental health and gardening. It has become more vital during times like this, with a worldwide pandemic and all the gloom about. The Royals can connect with a lot of people and have a positive influence on society, by promoting the positive health effects of being outdoors and specifically in the gardens. I enjoyed watching Prince Williams's documentary called the Backyard Nature Project. It was highly informative and I have further researched his project online.

From all this above and the pieces I've read on gardening and mental health, I'm even more keen to make our allotment fun and different, appealing for all who pass by and super for us who care for it.

N is for Nature

Without Nature, the world would be a very different place. We need nature to provide us with food we eat, the air we breathe and the water we irrigate the plants with. A vital part of growing our own food is respecting nature and using as man natural resources as possible. The title of our social media page is Allotment – Learn, Mend and Make do, and we have certainly abided by this. There are several items we had to purchase new, such as weed membrane, but the majority has been reclaimed, recycled and a lot of 'making-do'.

Having read that a really good resource for encouraging nature is a pond area, we thought we would make our own. With space being restricted and knowledge being limited, we started small. Having been given a large round, shallow plastic planter, we thought it would be ideal to use as the pond liner. The boys dug a whole deep enough, and we buried the planted up to the rim. Alfie lined the pond with some split logs, and upturned pots which will hopefully provide some little nooks for the frogs, newts and any other critter than decides to make our pond area home. To keep the water reasonably clear, we added some Oxygenating weed that a friend gave us, and a little ramp made of logs to enable access to wildlife. A final touch was a solar water fountain, which keeps the water from getting stagnant, as well as looking and sounding pretty. We have been told It can take approximately 12 months for a pond to become established, and we cannot wait!

The compost bins are located in one corner of the plot, and the children chose this area to keep as natural as possible. We have avoided cutting the grass around the bins, leaving it long for the insects to use. Around the bins, the boys placed some more split logs, which make ideal homes for all manner of creatures. The more insects we can encourager to the allotment, the more likely are crops are to get pollinated.

There are many things that can be done to assist the local wildlife, such as leaving some of the sunflower heads attached at the end of their flowering period. The birds will happily feast on the dried sunflower seeds and the insects enjoy the foliage as it dies back. As we had several sunflower heads, we took some home and hung them in our bird feeder by the window. It was lovely to watch the vast array of birds enjoying them, including Blue Tits, Robins, Blackbirds and Pigeons. After Halloween, we left out a couple of Pumpkins to be enjoyed by the birds and bugs. Although we made sure they were left out of reach from Hedgehogs, as they can have detrimental effects on their little digestive systems. Hedgehog numbers are already on the decline, so it is even more important to look after carefully.

Rather than cutting back our Strawberries and Raspberries straight away, we left them for the birds and bugs to ramble through and the Hedgehog has been seen clearing away the rotten Strawberries that we have left behind. A little Shrew was seen hiding in the flower garden and I am sure we have field mice hiding somewhere too.

Unfortunately, for reasons that they cannot help, we have tried not to encourage the birds into the allotment. I do provide plenty for them at home though. The birds enjoy eating our fruits and seedlings especially so we would rather they did not make a habit of attending the plot. To deter the birds we have used blank

CDs hung up, as the birds do not like the reflective material. We have also invested in some little wind spinners, as the movement and noise they create puts the birds off landing.

A few other plot holders and I are developing an empty plot into a communal area, which we hope to add a Polytunnel to. There are a few old crates erected in the middle of this plot, which we need to turn into a composting system. Though, the wasps have made an amazing nest in there at the moment, which we have chosen to leave until they naturally die off in the colder weather. It is important for us to work with nature rather than against, and there is no hurry to get the composting area started.

Being so close to nature has been a really easy way to teach the children about animals, habitats and more. Not a day goes by when they do not stumble across a new insect, a new batch of eggs hidden on leaves, a new creature's burrow in the ground. Another way in which the Allotment has assisted in home learning through the Lockdown period.

O is for Organic

Being an Organic gardener is not something I intentionally set out to do, but it just so happens that is my morals are in fact of the Organic way. The important things to me, such as avoiding synthetic fertilisers and pest control, recycling and keeping the plot as natural as possible are all the umbrella of being Organic.

The first step to becoming Organic can be properly treated soil. It is just as important for plants to get slot of nutrients, as well as us. The soil when we arrived on the allotment was good, having been left to its own device for a year or so. There were no areas that had been over worked and did not seem to be any sign of chemicals having been used. A simple way to tell this, is by digging a foot deep and taking note of the number of worms in the soil. Chemical soil treatments can harm the worms, as well as beneficial bacteria and other micro-organisms. You can also buy a PH testing kit, which will give you a complete breakdown of the nutrient levels in the soil. The boys helped analyze ours by using the digging method, they found lots of worms and even named a few.

To aid the quality of the soil, you can add Organic compost which is extremely easy to make. Our compost bin was half full of well-rotted manure and grass clippings when we arrived, so I was lucky enough to be able to use this straight away. But we have continued to top of the compost bins with any spare fruit and veg from meals, manure, spent plants, shredded paper and such like. Compos tis known as 'Black Gold' as it keeps food and garden waste out of landfills.

A lot of the plants from garden centres are labelled to display whether they have been grown using chemical fertilisers and pesticides, making them simple to avoid. We chose a lot of seedlings and seeds for our allotment, many of which had come from other organic growers on our site. Many things are best grown from seed anyway, such as Squash, Cucumbers, Sweet Peas and Sunflowers.

To avoid the need for any type of pest control, planting productively can make such a difference. Plants can be grouped tightly in beds, which reduces weeding and water waste. Ample space between rows can also help air circulation which repels fungal attacks. Using mulches can also reduce the number of weeds, due to blocking their access to sunlight.

No matter how hard we tried, we still had weeds appear and we pulled these by hand. By doing this little and often, we managed to keep fairly on top of it. One weed that is persistent on out plot, is Fat Hen. Although, we have learnt that Fat Hen can be harvested and eaten a bit like Quinoa. Perhaps this is a good weed to have after all.

There are a variety of Organic weapons that can be used on pests and bacteria's, such as horticultural oils, insecticidal soaps, garlic, and hot pepper sprays. We found soap and water a good mix to banish Flea Beetle and Aphids and keep a bottle made up in the shed.

Overall, Organic Gardening is amazing to help prevent the loss of topsoil, which is greatly affecting the planet. It also helps prevent water pollution, soil contamination, self-poisoning, death of insects, birds, critters, and other beneficial soil organisms. The children have made numerous comments regarding how the homegrown foods taste much fresher and some taste extremely different to those from a supermarket. This maybe down to less fungicide residues on foods from the synthetic fertilisers.

Science has proven that there are many health benefits from organic food, as well as the taste being nicer. Organic foods are rich in nutrients such as Vitamin C, Iron, Magnesium and Phosphorus. Organic crop-based food such as bread are up to 60% higher in many key antioxidants. These additional antioxidants are the equivalent of between 1-2 extra portions of fruit and vegetables a day. For the children to be consuming all this goodness without even realising is an extra bonus!

P is for Pollinators

As a girl, I was petrified of any insect that flutters and flies and even now, I have a phobia of moths. The Allotment though, has shown both the children and me, how important these critters are. I never knew that some plants grow a Male and Female flower, which need to Pollinate each other to grow healthy fruits. The most common way this occurs, is by the help of the insects.

I have seen on TV and media that the Bees are a vital part of humanity surviving, but I never knew exactly why. Approx. 80% of wildflowers in Europe require insect pollination, many of them rely solely on Bees. Bees also pollinate trees and bushes which are an important part of the ecosystem. A lot of animals and birds are dependent on these for food and shelter. Without the Bees, our supermarkets would have half the amount of fruit and vegetables.

There are more Pollinators than just Bees, a Pollinator is any animal that moves Pollen from the male flower to the female. So, we decided to dedicate an area of our Allotment to encourage as many pollinators as we can. This includes Bees, Butterflies, Wasps, Hoverflies, Moths and more.

The easiest way to encourage the Pollinators is to fill the area with flowers. Unlike the stereotypical Allotment, we had made a large sweeping flower bed across the front of ours. The boys have sprinkled all sorts of seeds, as well as planting all the bulbs and cuttings that we have been given. The stunning blue and orange cornflowers grew very quickly, but the majority will lay dormant until the next Spring. We are all excited to see how beautiful the flower bed will look. Some insects are active all year, so it will be nice to have something in bloom each season.

We heard on a television program about how to make a Bulb Lasagne. This entails layering different varieties of bulbs and compost into a container, so that after one bulb has bloomed, the next is already there waiting. It will be interesting to watch ours develop into a beautiful display.

There has been a new scheme arriving in some Garden Nurseries, which involves certain plants having a label with the image of a Bee on and these plants are especially good to attract the Bees. But in general, we have found out that most pollinators prefer pastel colour flowers which tend to live longer in the Summer heat.

The area to encourage the pollinators is around our compost bins, which we have left the grass uncut and added some split logs. This area will provide vital food as well as shelter. I have read that pollinator populations have been in decline since 1950's, largely due to the loss of their natural habitats.

As well as pollen, the insects require a home. By providing a little bug sanctuary, we can add a habitat solution.

The boys have made a couple of bug sanctuaries and locate them at various points throughout the allotment. We have up-turned pots which they have filled with twigs and leaves, as well as old plastic bottles filled with natural materials. From an old rabbit hutch, we were kindly given, we have made a larger Bug Sanctuary. It has tin cans filled with bamboo, bricks with holes for the solitary bees, stacks of leaves and twigs and piles of dead wood. We hope to see some critters living and laying their eggs in these sanctuaries soon.

Our pond will also be beneficial for the Pollinators. Not only are the plants we have in our pond good for pollinators, but the water has attracted some beautiful Dragonflies. We love to see the vast array of insects discovering the water source and hope to expand the pond in the future.

Q is for Quarantine

By now, the majority of people know what Quarantine means. To reduce the risk or catching or spreading Coronavirus, we have been advised to quarantine ourselves if we have symptoms. If we are not in quarantine, we are still to abide by the lockdown rules and not interact with other people indoors, avoid unnecessary travel and keep 2 metres away from everyone accept your own household.

There is no doubt that the restrictions during Lockdown have given many people a newfound love for the outdoors, with activities indoors being so restricted. The applications for Allotments have had a 500% increase in some areas of the UK. We were not the only ones who look forward to visiting the allotment during the bleakness of lockdown, as a poll by the Nation Trust found that 38% of adults in the UK agree. Being surrounded by nature has helped a lot of us through this difficult time.

It has been a blessing that throughout Lockdown, we have still been able to buy from online stores and a lot of the Garden Centres have offered a delivery service. We managed to purchase some potting soil from our local supermarket and order seeds from online stores.

Sadly, most of the plant fairs and flower events have been cancelled. However, there have been a lot of venues and events offering Virtual Tours and Video Links as an alternative. It has actually been easier for us to virtually immerse ourselves in these beautiful venues, that in ordinary life, we would not have been able to attend due to distance etc. My mum and I have booked a coach tour to the Chelsea Flower Show next year, which we have talked about attending for a long time. I really hope that Coronavirus has taken a nosedive by then, and the restrictions are lifted.

As well as public events and shows, we have also been restricted in celebrating causes and historical events. To celebrate Remembrance Day, we were not able to purchase the paper poppies like usual or gather at memorials to show our respects. Instead we  have shown our respects by adding diy poppies to the allotment. By cutting the bottom end off plastic bottles and spraying them red we have created a beautiful arrangement on a wooden stake to display. I also saw an idea to use a vinyl record and mould them into poppies. Simply warm the record up and allow it flex around a bowl, leaving a wavy floral shape when cooled. Paint the vinyl red and the centre black. We hung ours up on our shed and have received many compliments regarding it.

We were lucky to be offered an Allotment, as soon after our arrival, there was a waiting list for plots. Sadly, all the communal plots have been closed due to reducing the risk of contracting and spreading of the virus. For us, living in the countryside has been extremely beneficial, for allowing us access to clean, fresh air and open spaces. But I do wonder how those who live in urban areas, without gardens have managed. Shockingly the levels of attempted suicides in London have risen by 70% this year.

I have expressed how much the Allotment has improved both the children's and my mental health. Rather than being stuck inside without the normal routines, without being able to socialise as we normally do and without any idea of what our futures hold, we have been able to get outside in your own secure little area and fill our days with fun and unintentional learning.

There were a few days, when we had to quarantine ourselves due to showing symptoms of the virus and waiting for test results. Luckily, it was proven to be just colds and we were soon back to the Allotment. But during those days, the community at our site were amazing and keep a close eye on our crops whilst we could not. They were kind enough to water our beds for us and keep us updated on the crops progress through photos online.

It really has been a time to cement the value of nature and let us be thankful for the simple things in life. We now appreciate more than just the material things in life. With all this doom and gloom, it is lovely to see a positive side and embrace the situations thrust upon us.

R is for Roots

Before acquiring the Allotment, I had a basic knowledge that roots of plants were extremely important and the plant depends on them for survival. But other than that, I did not really know their vital role.

I can now confidently confirm, that after 5 months of gardening, Roots need a lot more consideration that just letting them get on with growing. The root systems vary hugely depending on the type of plant, this includes their depth requirements, their nutritional needs, what they can provide us and even what disease they can have.

The root systems take in Oxygen, water, and nutrients from the soil, to move them up through the plant to the stems, leaves, blooms and fruits. The roots store energy, and a good example of this is edible roots such as carrots, turnips and beets.

It is easy to compare a plant and its roots to the human being. When I am poorly, my body and mind show signs of this. When a plant is poorly, the leaves and blooms can show the signs. To find the reason behind the illness is to look at the roots, or in a human the organs. Healthy roots make a healthy plant!

Stress can cause plants problems, so when transplanting be incredibly careful to avoid damaging the root system. I learnt this when I planted my Celebration Squash plant. It was within a few days, that the leaves started to turn yellow and limp. My fellow Allotmenteer explained this was plant stress. As well as transplanting, plant stress can be caused through temperatures, water fluctuations, animal predation or disease.

Unfortunately, many weeds have extremely resistant roots, ensuring a long life considering they are often subject to munching from herbivores, mulching, lawn mowing and more. Weeds rapidly produce more foliage, after sacrificing the tops to save the roots.

I learnt quite early on that roots need room to grow, if they become compacted by lack of space, the plant will suffer and can result in the slowly of plant growth. I could not understand why one of my cucumber plants was producing luscious long cucumbers, but the other was not producing any. Until it suddenly dawned on me, that they had different sized pots and perhaps the smaller one had outgrown the pot. When I re-potted it, I could clearly see that the roots had grown out the drainage holes in the pot and were not able to grow productively.

The roots can also develop diseases, which can spell doom for the plants. Having learnt the hard way, excess water can cause detrimental problems. The water excess water and sometimes added warm temperatures can cause the roots to rot., which causes the plants to die. But too little water can also cause the plant to die, as their major food and oxygen supply dries out and dies.

There are some plant roots that are edible, such as kitchen staples like Onions, Potatoes and Garlic. Root vegetables contain many vitamins and minerals, eating a variety of them is great for your health. The children absolutely loved growing our potatoes and they can be used in such a variety of ways too. It has been proven by scientists that root vegetables help the gut bacteria, they lower high levels of blood fats and blood glucose and they reduce the risk of type 2 diabetes, heart disease and bowel cancer.

Several of the surrounding allotments are growing Turnips and Parsnips. I have not really used many of these when cooking, but it has prompted me to try and include a few more in our diet. The children are not too keen on soups, but we could use them in mash and casseroles.

Roots can also cause damage, as I learnt when I planted my buddleia to close to the house. My mum was quick to kindly point out that the root systems can be detrimental to buildings as they grow far and wide and through anything that gets in the way. So as swiftly as it was planted, it was dug up again and repositioned behind a bench in the allotment.

It has been surprising how far some roots travel. I was attempting to thin out the raspberry canes in the fruit cage, but I had not bargained on the roots going so deep and for such a distance. It seemed that the more I pulled at one cane, the more it dislodged others. Eventually I succumbed to just trimming them back and hoping they do not spread so quickly next year.

S is for Soil

I have always thought of soil as a brown, smelly looking material found in the garden. As far as I knew, it was used to feed plants and that was about its only purpose. Little did I know!

Recently I watched a program about how we can improve the quality of the soil; it was rated highly by friends and I thought I would give it a go. After the program, I was left stunned at how important the soil is and how quickly it is being depleted. According to Scientists, we have approx. 60 years until the world runs out of topsoil! That is just 60 years of Harvests.

History has shown that the main cause of soil degrading is due to tillage; a process used by farmers which removes carbon from the soil and releases into the air as carbon dioxide. Some farmers use excessive amounts of fertilisers and pesticides and some overgraze their animals, which exposes the carbon in the soil. Thanks to conventional farming practices, it is hopeful that the soil erosion can be reduced, and farmers are more aware of the damage that has been caused. Nearly half of the most productive soil in the world has disappeared in the last 150 years.

Soil can influence the climate on a smaller scale. The wetter the soil or denser will hold heat more than drier and looser soil. If soil continues to affect the earth so dramatically, we may not be able to grow plants and trees, meaning we would not eb able to survive. The banning of certain pesticides and the reduction in others, as well as less farmers using tilling is hopefully going to see a dramatic decline in the amount of soil damage within the next few years.

This Lockdown period has increased the amount of Allotments being desired and therefore the amount of land that is now being cultivated. It is evidently visible on our site, that most plot holders are using the No Dig method when it comes to prepping their beds.

Unintentionally, the boys and I decided to use the 'No-dig' method. This was more through laziness and heat exhaustion in the Summer, than through knowledge of soil prevention schemes. Rather than spend a long time digging our beds, we simply built a frame from reclaimed timber and added compost, topsoil, paper, and grass clippings to create ourselves a vegetable bed.

Having clay soil at our allotment means that during the Autumn and Winter we have largely flooded areas and it is very sticky under foot. Because of this, the No Dig method is better to cope with extreme weather as it provides better soil drainage and better soil conservation.

The 'No Dig' method provides a rich soil to grow in and is also great for suppressing weeds. The soil becomes more stable as it is not disrupted by digging including disrupting the micro-organisms, fungi and worms. The boys have positively relished in the huge quantity of worms we found living in the vegetable beds.

We are hoping that by growing in the beds we have made this Autumn we will have plants that grow to their full potential with more nutritional crops. Over a couple of days, I have moved over a ton of topsoil and another of manure by hand into the raised beds and then covered with a weed suppressing membrane. We are trying to improve the soil quality as best we can.

When purchasing any soil, remember to enquire about where it has come from and what it includes. Some top-soils are not very nutritious as they are simply leftovers from garden renovations or building works. They can be full of rubble, stones and debris that may negatively affect your crops. We have a supplier near to the allotment site who provides us with a good quality topsoil at a discounted rate. The soil is mixed with a compost already and very nutritional. It has also been sieved to remove any unwanted contaminants.

As well as using the soil on the vegetable beds, we use it on our vertical gardens too. Along the fence we have a couple of material shoe racks which we filled with soil and added strawberry runners to. These are great for increasing the space in which we can plant but also for adding height to the plot and making a more visual experience. However, when the water hits the top pocket, it runs through the soil and down into the next and then the next. It does mean all the plants get watered, but it can also mean the water easily washes away any nutrients that the top pockets contain. It is vital for us to replenish these nutrients in order for the plants to reach their full potential.

T is for tools

It was bittersweet that I was gifted a lot of garden tools from my husband's late grandad, although it has made it extra special being able to put them into good use again. My dad also gave me some tools, including a power drill and saw. The variety of tools have all been equally useful, from the hand spade to plant, with to the saw which I used to make the raised beds.

When we started we just had a few hand tools, including a spade, fork, rake and hand trowel. Most of these I knew how to use and put straight to work making beds and digging the weeds. The children have equally had fun with the hand tools, using them to help me and also digging for worms.

Assuming I knew how to use these hand tools, I was surprised to learn that there are in fact several types of spades and rakes. The most common spade is a garden spade, which typically has a long handle and is wide and has parts to drive the spade into the ground. There is a similar spade but with a thinner head, called an Irish spade and one with a narrower spade called a sharpshooter. The garden spade is used for digging and breaking up the soil, whereas the sharpshooter spade is used for shovelling the soil.

The rake come as a lawn rake, which has long tines that fan out and then there is the garden rake, which has wide set, short tines. The lawn rakes can be used for a variety of tasks such as picking up leaves and debris without penetrating the soil beneath and the garden rake is used for moving, spreading, and levelling soil. A little bit of advice is to make sure you avoid standing on the end of the rake, as it will flip up and bop you on the nose. I found this out the hard way and at the point that the neighbouring plots were being tended to. There was laughter all round and I was left with a sore nose and blushing cheeks.

Another tool I was surprised to find there were so many types of is the garden hoe. Hoes are traditionally used to cultivate the soil and remove the weeds. I have what is called a Dutch hoe. It has a shallow angled blade with a front cutting edge and I use it to weed between seedlings and dig shallow trenches for seeds to be sown. There are many other types such as the draw hoe and warren hoe, each with their own uses. Living on the lockdown budget we have managed by just using our Dutch hoe, but I wonder if life could be made easier if I invested in some more varieties.

Having had two previous knee surgeries and awaiting two more, I am very aware that I need to protect my joints whilst working at the allotment. One of the first purchases I made was a couple of kneeling pads which consist of foam pads to provide a cushion when kneeling. These have proven invaluable and we have all made use of them. I have also seen in the shops that taller and more sturdy kneelers are available, including ones you can sit on and ones with wheels.

Some simple tools such as scissors, shears, trowels and forks have been especially useful. The most used items would have to be the gardening gloves and wheelbarrow, for obvious reasons. The hose pipe has been essential, especially in the hot Summer months. I thought I had found a bargain hose pipe at a particularly good price and free delivery. The only problem was when it arrived it was a lot shorted than I had envisaged, it would seem I got my feet and metres muddled! Our plot is the furthest away from the communal taps and to reach we needed fifty metres but my bargain came at fifty feet instead. The husband found this very amusing!

I am still a great advocate for using hands as they are the best tool we could have and they are free to use. Almost any task can be completed with the use of hard graft and our hands. The hard graft comes at a cost, as many days I have been left aching and burnt out, but after all the work getting the allotment started this year it should pay off and be easier next year.

To help with my aches and back pains, I invested in an acupuncture massaging mat. The mat consists of strategically placed treatment points, that stimulate muscle relaxation nerve and blood flow. I can honestly say that this mat has been hugely valuable in helping me almost instantly recover and often I have had to fight the children to use it. I think it should be in the top ten recommended tools for gardeners.

U is for Unusual

When someone says they have an allotment the Peter Rabbit style image springs to mind, a rectangular patch of dirt with lots of vegetables growing in pretty rows. Our allotment is as far from this stereotypical style and is instead more of a garden with pretty patches of flowers and vegetable beds located in various shapes and sizes.

As Alfie has additional requirements to the other children I wanted to make the allotment fun and more enticing for him. One of the first things I set-up was the Sensory Herb Spiral. A spiral of bricks that get higher towards the middle and a variety of herbs planted within. These range from Lemon Balm, Curry Plant, Mint, Rosemary and more. The insects enjoy it just as much as we do and Alfie loves to be hands-on and smell all the different scents as well as touch the varying textures.

The two flower beds that sweep across either end of the plot are beautiful and we receive a lot of compliments regarding these. Whilst it is important for us to cultivate the land we also want to spend our time enjoying the plot. We take picnics and books and spend time relaxing as well as gardening, the flowers give us and the wildlife something to appreciate.

Whilst I chose to sit and relish my picnic on the table and chairs, the children have their own little den to sit in. We made this from a pallet as the base and used cot sides are the walls. These also convert into trellis for the beans to climb up. Inside the den the children have a tough tray filled with soil and little ornaments, such as fairies and animals. I quite often find Alfie sitting in here playing with the ornaments.

There is plenty to see and do in our allotment, such as the animated windsocks, a fish and a dragon. We have little windmills, decorative pots and plenty of garden ornaments scattered throughout. There is bunting across the shed, wind chimes that we made from tin cans and our gorgeous looking DIY scarecrows. The allotment is as much a place of fun as well as a place to grow food.

The very first thing we made for the Allotment was a little scarecrow named Phillip. He was made from a stuffed pillowcase, with wool for hair and Alfie's old shorts and t-shirt. He was extremely cute but not very secure as he was perched on just two flimsy canes. As much as we adore Phillip and he quickly became part of our family, he needed a sturdier friend. Along came Jemima, a rather sassy scarecrow we made using a timber cross and screwing a dress and straw hat to it. She has woven gloves and a playful belt. Her face however, needed a couple of attempts.

Initially, I drew her face onto the wooden cross with pens and sprayed it with a varnish coating. She looked great and we loved her. After tea, we popped outside to tidy up the garden before bath time and Alfie made a comment that the scarecrow was scary. I didn't think she was, I loved her smiley face. I could have jumped a millions miles when I turned to glance at her and saw the most frightful looking image. Alfie was right, she looked terrifying, as the varnish layer had made the ink of her eyes run and stream down her face like a demented clown! Plan B, I re-drew her happy, smiling face onto a plastic picnic plate and secured it on top of the rather scary looking one. Once again, she was beautiful and now has pride of place attached to a fence post in the middle of the plot.

I like to be creative so I made some little clay creatures and hid them throughout the plot. The children and their friends from neighbouring plots enjoy finding them all and learning little facts about them. To me, there is a great importance in getting youth to engage with the outdoors and if they can learn through having fun, it becomes a winning situation.

Part of the reason behind writing this book is to encourage others to use their land to meet their own requirements and not necessarily feel pressured into following the mainstream. When I first told people, we were going to use our allotment as a garden as well as growing crops, I was met with conflicting views. The majority pulled an awkward face, some tried to convince me that adding flowers was not permitted and others questioned that we were even allowed to visit an allotment for fun and enjoyment and they were just for cultivating crops. It has been quite fulfilling to see that almost every one of those people has had their views on allotments changed and can see what a beautiful space we have created.

You do not even need to have an allotment to grow food and enjoy the space, many use their own gardens and balconies to do exactly that.

V is for Variety

Having never grown my own food before, I was not aware that there is so much variety when it comes to seeds. My first shock was when I had a seed catalogue delivered and discovered three pages purely based on carrot seeds! I soon realised that some clever people have spent years perfecting all these types of seeds, including ones that are disease free, ones that can be planted at differing times of the year, different sized crops and much more.

To my delight I was able to purchase seeds that were able to give a novice like me a better chance of growing the best crops possible. A lot of these seeds are known as F1 hybrid seeds. An F1 hybrid means the result of breeding two different strains of a variety to produce a third variety. Plants grown from F1 hybrid seeds tend to grow stronger and have greater survival rates but they are often much more expensive.

A cheaper alternative to buying seeds can be to save seeds. There are many seeds you can save and re-plant, including potatoes and sunflowers. Although some do not grow true and the plants are nothing like the parent plant. Pumpkins are a prime example, as they can easily cross-pollinate, resulting in some unusual crops in future plants.

I have seen in supermarkets the vast array of salad leaves and lettuces but I have never come across half the varieties that I have gained free from magazines. They seem to come in all sizes and colours, from sweet to peppery. I think that a lot of them I will grow as experiments to work out our favourite flavours.

The supermarkets are a great place to explore the varieties of food available, although a lot have racked up some airmiles by being grown abroad in warmer climates.

After reading some books on growing at home I now know that there are certain varieties of plant better for beginners. Rather than attempting to grow every seedling you are given, like we did, it is apparently easier to concentrate on some simple crops and when you have more knowledge and experience, then expand into other varieties. As we got our allotment late in the year we jumped straight in and had a go with everything. To be honest, I found this method worked for us, as we learnt a lot as we went along and had no choice but to do a lot of research to achieve what we have. There was no backing down when we went from grass to over twenty varieties growing within four months.

It has been nice to start with such a lot in our first year, as we have a fair understanding of what worked well for us and what to concentrate on next year. I know not to waste time attempting to grow a lot of brassicas as they just did not work for us. We also had far too many courgettes and tomatoes, so know that next year we can cut back on those and make room for more potatoes as we did not have enough of those.

The children have discovered that there are different varieties of their favourite crops, such as the sweetcorn and pumpkins. It is lovely to encourage their desire to grow more and to try different variations, so we have bought some seeds to grow Polar White Pumpkins and Jewel Sweet corn in the coming year.

We did have some surprises when it came to our peppers this Summer. We were given some healthy green seedlings and told they were peppers. We were excited as we enjoy peppers in a variety of ways, such as snacking on and adding to stir-fry and Bolognese dishes. However, much to our dismay these pepper plants turned out to be of the chilli pepper variety and I had to convince the children that they would not like to snack on those! They were put to good use still and we shared them with a friend who relishes spicy food!

W is for Weather

The most important part of growing your own food is the weather! The weather can make the difference between an extremely poor harvest or a brilliant one. You can plan and prepare for almost every incident but the weather always has the ultimate decision. We learnt this after planting some bulbs into beautiful dry soil but losing them to floods a day later.

If the weather gets too cool, plant yields will be reduced and they may not grow at all. We had problems with the tomatoes ripening towards the end of the Summer as the weather quickly became very cool and there was not enough warmth or light to inhibit pigment synthesis. We ended up harvesting all the green tomatoes and bringing them home to ripen. Having been advised that the best way to ripen them is to place them in a breathable container with a banana. The banana releases ethylene gas which promotes ripening.

The rain this year has been plentiful to the point that the clay soil on allotment became like glue! Some seeds such as our carrots failed to germinate in the wet soil and the slugs ravaged our brassicas. It is nigh on impossible to plant out into the sodden soil as this can rot the roots and bulbs. The heavy rain can also leach nutrients in the soil which will affect the plants growth.

Although heavy rains and overcast weather is not really appreciated by us gardeners, the clouds do help protect the tender seedlings from the harsh sun. It is a bittersweet feeling when the clouds are about as they can affect the process of photosynthesis. Some plants have evolved their own cloud protection called photoprotection. When it is shaded the leaves effectively switch off and then turn back on when the sun returns.

There is no shade on our allotment so we need to be careful with regards to sun scorch and sometimes appreciate the odd cloudy day through Summer. The full sunlight scorched our cucumber plants by causing oxidation – the equivalent to sunburn. Mostly the plants grow faster when they receive more sunlight, with the majority requiring approximately six hours of sunlight a day.

I recently discovered that growing your crops in rows north to south is preferential over those grown east to west. This is because the rows tend to shade each other, and they do not get enough sun exposure.

allotment suffers greatly from being exposed. The wind whips across the site and we have all suffered wind damage at some point this year. As well as my mix of greenhouses, the sweetcorn and tomatoes have been bent, the cold frame has been dismantled, the bean den collapsed, the shed doors have blown open and pots have been tossed around like candy floss.

Along one side of the plot we added a wind shield material. This was cheap and made a huge difference, although I have now noticed that the farmer has harvested the maize surrounding the allotments and we now receive wind from all directions. The maize was obviously offering us a little wind protection from across the fields. Other than tying everything down within an inch of its life we just need to be careful. There is a no gas policy on site and I can now understand why.

X is for Xeriscaping and Irrigation

Xeriscaping isn't a word commonly heard but there aren't many other gardening terms beginning with X. The term Xeriscaping is when you design an outside area to reduce or eliminate the need for irrigation, using only water that the natural climate provides. During the Summer months when we first took on our Allotment there were daily queues for the tap to water our plants. I could easily spend a good couple of hours in the evening making sure all the flowers and plants had a good soaking, as the soil seemed so dry. However, the Autumn has brought along completely different problems when it comes to the soil.

After the first weekend of rain in October it was soon noticeably clear that our soil is actually very sticky clay and does not allow good drainage of the water. The beds were full of puddles and my wellies got amusingly stuck at one point. It was a comical tug of war with the pathway and my boots!

Having two such different experiences with regards to the irrigation on our Allotment, it has bought with it some utter confusion and made me feel rather unsettled about how to deal with this. During the Summer I have concentrated on mulching the beds with grass clippings and rotted manure to retain as much moisture as possible, but now I am aerating and adding topsoil to discourage the moisture retention.

It was important to get the watering requirements for the plants correct as it is a vital part of growing healthy plants that reach their full potential. Watering in the evenings allowed the plants to soak up most of the water before the sun and evaporation occurring throughout the day. When watering larger and thirstier plants like the Squash and Pumpkins, it is handy to half bury a bottle with drainage holes next to the plant. By doing this and adding the water directly into the bottle, it allows it to soak down straight to the roots and avoids any surface water loss.

We were kindly given a water butt when we first arrived on the plot and I have located this next to the shed to catch the runoff rain. This was brilliant in the Summer to provide a quick access to fresh rainwater, which was used to water the plants that just needed a little extra and were not dry to the touch. During the much hotter days I used our 50metre long hose attached to the communal tap to drench all the beds. I was advised that watering the soil and roots directly was much better for the plants than showering the foliage, as this can cause rot and encourage mold to grow.

One of our investments was a beautiful half barrel, which was previously used for Whiskey and was already treated and watertight. We filled this up with water and covered with a mesh to prevent any creatures drowning. This 'pond like' feature is ideal for dipping pots in to soak the roots and give them a good drink. The plants in the greenhouse are sat in small trays which we can add water to that can be sucked up by the roots.

Some days, if we knew we could not make it to the allotment we would use a drip feed to water the plants. This involves quickly turning over a full bottle of water and plunging it into the soil. The water slowly leaks out of the bottle as the soil dries out. It meant the plants still got their feed without us having to be there.

I think in the Summer months, most of our time was spent watering the allotment and then watering ourselves as the heat wore us out! It became a vital part of the week, planning our time to make sure the plants were thriving.

A-Z OF ALLOTMENT GARDENING

Y is for Youths

Results have shown that outdoor learning has provided opportunities for youths to develop in some major areas. As well as improving interpersonal relationship skills, gardening can positively contribute to developing behavioral competence, contributions to the community, construction skills, responsibilities and much more.

One such improvement I have seen in our three boys has been the nutritional values. The children have never been fussy eaters, but they do seem much more inclined to try new foods knowing they have grown it themselves. They have been keen to eat straight from the plants and have even asked to grow specific varieties in our next season.

I believe that growing their own foods has promoted their self-confidence due to achieving their goals and reaping the rewards of their hard work. Many times, they have talked to their extended family and friends about the food they have grown, how they have nurtured seeds and made meals from their efforts.

Giving youths a responsibility, such as caring for plants also provides them with a perfect combination of skills. For example, over the Lockdown period the children had limited access to sports facilities and outdoor areas but by gardening they have developed their physical skills. For younger children, gardening helps improve their fine motor skills and coordination.

I have spoken briefly about the sensory stimulation that you can experience from the outdoors, the feeling of different textured plants, the water, the smells and sounds. We have made our allotment a visual explosion by planting all the colours of the rainbow in the flower beds and adding pops of colour through the decorative ornaments. Alfie has a condition called Autism, which in his case means he has some sensory issues. Being at the allotment has really helped him overcome some of his sensory fears including embracing new textures and accepting the movement of creatures in his hands. There have been times where Alfie has worn headphones to eliminate overpowering sounds but he has become intrigued by the new sounds at the plot. This includes the noisy combine harvester in the field next door and the airplanes taking off from the airport close by.

The older boys have used and improved their literacy skills through choosing plants, reading instructions and writing out the labels. Alfie has been using sticks to make letter formations in the soil and drawing shapes with flints on the concrete slabs.

All of us have increased our intellectual skills, learning through the processes of preparing, planting, nurturing and harvesting. We have often discussed the plants and various topics concerning the allotment. The children relish in telling their dad all the things they have learnt when he gets home from work. Once lockdown was lifted a little and they returned to school they asked to take in photos and samples of the plants and crops that they have been learning about to share with their classes.

Our Allotment is an adventure for the children, from the mud kitchen and pond area, to the hopscotch and bean den. During periods of relaxed lockdown, we have had the other children on the site in our plot, discovering and learning along side the boys. Research has shown that children perform better at school if they have been involved in gardening. All three of the boys have wildlife gardens at their schools and the infant school even has its own polytunnel.

In 2019, we celebrated 80 years since Dig for Victory. This was a time when children were required to cultivate the land with their parents and elders, taking on the tasks of weeding and gathering. In 1830, it was thought that one eighth of an acre would feed a family of five! Three quarters of the space was commonly devoted to potatoes and the rest to cabbages, parsnips and beans, all staple foods still found in allotments today. In 1939, when the Dig for Victory campaign was born, growing food became a patriotic duty. In my opinion, a lot of today's youth have lost this ability to live off the land. With so many supermarkets supplying much more exotic foods and convenience food at its prime, there is less requirements for people to be able to grow their own food.

I have absolutely revelled in teaching the children how to be self-sufficient and love to see them teaching their peers, be it through sharing what they have learnt verbally, demonstrating at school how to sow seeds and by sharing the food they have grown.

The most valuable part of youths getting involved in the outdoors is working together, building bonds this Summer with the children has created some fantastic memories for us all. The boys have learnt skills that will benefit them lifelong and I have learnt so much more about them as individuals. I really hope we make lots more memories in the years to come.

Z is for Zones

The latest lesson I have learnt is the technical term for the area I am growing in, a zone. It was not until I joined some social media gardening groups from around the world, that I realised that plant growth and survival is relevant to climatic conditions within a certain geographical area, a zone.

The UK lies in plant hardiness zones 6 through to 9, with variations occurring between regions and seasons. Here in Norfolk UK, I am growing in zone 8a. Our Summers are cooler than those on the continent, never really reaching above 33° C but the Winters are a lot milder. Around our coastal areas February is usually the coldest month but inland there is little difference between January and February.

The UK's frost-free growing season is long and mostly starts in March to April and ending with the first frosts in November. This means that most of the food is grown outdoors during the Summer months in the UK but it is not limited to just these months with the use of greenhouses, poly tunnels and cloches.

Your growing zone is an important factor when purchasing new plants and deciding which ones are likely to thrive. Some plants would not survive a cold Winter in the UK and therefore a greenhouse is a favourite for a lot of gardeners. The greenhouse allows us to grow plants that would otherwise not survive, by growing in a warmer environment.

Due to having cold Winters and warm Summers in our zone a lot of seeds and bulbs can only be planted at certain times of the year. Some can go straight into the ground outside and others can be started off in a warmer greenhouse and then planted outside when they are seedlings.

When I planted out my tomatoes in June we were still having a few chilly nights so I decided to cover the immature plants with a cold frame overnight to give them the best chance of surviving. The cold weather can cause the water in the plant cells to freeze,  damaging the cell wall. Roots are also unable to take water up and the plant dies due to lack of moisture.

There are some crops that benefit from a frost, such as Garlic, Green onions, Swiss Chard and Leeks. The flavour of these is improved by exposure to a spell of below freezing temperature. Other plants like Peppers, Squash, Beans and Okra can be covered with a fleece blanket in frosts to protect their tender leaves and fruits.

Taking all this into consideration I have found it is also important to consider where the plant originates from and the drought tolerance. For example, an Alpine species will cope much better with extreme heat than a native bog plant. We are still trying to decide on a variety of fruit tree to plant that will suit all the requirements of Zone 8a but in clay soil and in a windy area. There is so much to consider when trying to achieve the highest potential of the plants.

GLOSSARY

ADHD – A condition effecting people's behaviour

Allotment – A plot of land rented by an individual for crowing vegetables or flowers

Allotmenteer – A person who grows crops in an allotment

Autism – A developmental disorder of variable severity

Bolt – When a plant produces flowers or seeds at the detriment of the edible crop.

Brassica – Members of the Cabbage family

Climatise – Acclimate to a new environment

Cloche – A transparent cover temporarily used to protect crops

Coldframe – A low structure used to shelter crops

Compost – A product of decomposed materials

Covid 19 (Coronavirus) – Sever acute respiratory syndrome

Fertiliser – A chemical or natural substance added to oil to increase its fertility

Furlough – Leave of absence

Germinate – The process of seeds becoming seedlings

Harvest – The process of gathering crops

Lockdown – The confining of people in order to reduce the number of Coronavirus cases

Mulch – A layer of material on the surface of soil

Nutrients – A substance that provides nourishment essential for growth

Organic – When produced without the use of artificial chemicals

Pest – Destructive insect or other animal that attacks crops

Pollinate – The transfer of pollen to allow a plant to allow fertilisation

Quarantine – A period in isolation

Seedling – A young plant raised from seed or a cutting

Social Media – Websites and Applications that enable us to share content and participate in networking

Weed – A wild plant growing where it is not wanted

Xeriscape – Process of gardening that eliminates the need for supplemental water

Acknowledgments

I would firstly like to thank my Husband Marc and our 3 boys, George, Harry, and Alfie. Their participation and patience in getting our Allotment to where it is now has been incredible. I have had their support and encouragement all the way and could not have done any of this without them.

Secondly, my family have been tremendous. They have offered invaluable advice and helped me, from gathering freebies, to digging the weeds. Dad and Ann who put up the shed and provided me with power tools, my mum has given me the majority of our flowers and assisted me in the planning along the way, my Nanny who has helped me purchasing the greenhouse and encouraged me, my Parents In-law who have also provided some hand tools and they've all done so much more in between.

My friends, fellow Allotmenteers and our local community who have been incredibly supportive and given us lots of freebies and seedlings to get us started.

Not forgetting all the followers on my Social Media page, who have given me the inspiration and encouragement to carry on. They have shared their ideas and advice; they have offered kind words and have motivated me along the journey, and they have made it all worth while seeing the love they also share for our Allotment.

Printed in Great Britain
by Amazon